DEDICATION

This book is dedicated to all those finding their voice.
To those who think their life doesn't matter,
may this book illuminate how it does.

CONTENTS

YOU CAN'T SEE WHAT I CAN SEE

A Foreword

Socially, audacity is an oft-admonished concept, but it is also the only means by which certain objectives become realized. Early last year, when the Dean's Office solicited suggestions for my college's speaker's series, I threw in Ta-Nehisi Coates as his essay "The Case for Reparations" was necessary reading for the nation in 2014—especially those of us obsessed with deducing how exactly we have arrived at this point in American history. I never expected the administration to take my recommendation seriously, let alone actually offer Mr. Coates an appropriate honorarium to come (—the audacity—), but they did. The event was successful in ways I could not have anticipated, especially in the manner that Mr. Coates' candor and incisive analysis spoke to the experiences of our campus' small "black" student population.

He made one short yet profound point that I believe is important to keep in mind as you encounter these Ballou students' testimonies and poems, that being that there is nothing inherently wrong with "black" people—particularly the oft-maligned urban "black" population. "What is novel about that," you might ask. Well, "black power" and "black is beautiful" are statements that come out people's mouths as easily as the pathologizing tropes of "hood" and "bama." (In fact, I would say that is how the term "ghetto" often operates in the "black" imagination—as representative of the majesty of, or in spite of, disenfranchisement and struggle.) But from the external perspective, shared by many of those who claim to care for young "black" children and make the policy decisions that shape their lives, these students' "blackness" is perceived as something that needs to be fixed, corrected. This is not true. There is nothing about these children and their struggles that can or should be explained solely by their culture and ethnicity.

How the broader society—teachers, police officers, mayors, congressional representatives and presidents—chooses to engage with them and their culture is another matter.

There is a sad "you" that haunts this book:
"When I went to sit down next to you, lady, you looked scared."
"You don't know me, so you don't know who I am."
"You think I am stuck in Southeast and I'm never going to go anywhere."
"You think you know why we sell drugs."
"You say we don't care about anyone but ourselves… What about you. Do you care about us?"

If you read this book, you have to ask yourself how often you are within this "you" these students are evoking. The dismissive you. The resigned you. The judgmental or spooked you. You may even have your rationales for why you have been "you" at different points in your life, but a rationale makes none of it justified.

These children—they are children—do not deserve to meet and face and battle that "you" every day, but they must—in addition to fending off depression or raising siblings at the expense of their own childhoods and educations or surviving in homes with the barest of staples. All of those burdens are more than enough to juggle while striving for a realized future. The psychological weight of being criminalized and demonized (literally, lest we forget the testimony of Darren Wilson) in the American imagination only exacerbates what it means to grow up in the far eastern edge of the nation's capital.

Despite all they encounter that announces, if not trumpets, "we do not care," they have written their stories and feelings for this book. An act of audacity, I would say. You can reward their audacity by reading what is here and humanizing yourself. If their writing elicits no frustration or shame in you, you may still be wearing the veil of "you." They are not waiting for you to divest— they have too much to do—but they would welcome the occasion.

—*Kyle G. Dargan*
Associate Professor,
Literature and Creative Writing
American University

PREFACE

We began this second year of the Ballou Story Project with the same mission as the first: to help students capture powerful stories about their lives that demonstrated their character, their resilience, their dreams. Writers use these pieces as personal statements for scholarships and college applications. There is no time when stakes are higher to tell your story with power and grace.

But this was during a heavy year of high stakes, and of even higher emotion. During the summer before these writers began this school year, Mike Brown was shot in Ferguson, and crowds took to the streets, angry about yet another unarmed black man killed by police. Later that fall, when the grand jury did not find the officer at fault, the streets erupted again— this time across the country—demanding justice from a system that regularly brutalized black bodies. Then came Eric Garner. Then Tamir Rice. John Crawford. Sean Bell.

It became clear that this was a historic time, a new chapter in our country's ongoing Civil Rights Movement. These writers wanted to be part of it, to have a voice in this powerful national conversation about race, inequality, violence, and justice. So we re-focused the project's mission and connected to a Movement. And rather than simply offer reactions to events, these writers wanted to do more: they wanted to Change the Narrative

about young people of color. For them the #BlackLivesMatter movement resonates not only for its outcry against police violence, but more broadly, as a humanizing, rallying cry for dignity and respect. And if you know these writers—really know the stories of their lives—you cannot help but afford them that due regard. For that reason, we decided to create our own Riot of Voices.

In our final month of writing, Walter Scott was shot eight times in the back while running away from a cop in North Charleston. Two days before our final photo shoot, the nearby city of Baltimore burned. After days of peaceful protests demanding answers from the Baltimore police for the unexplained death of Freddie Gray, the frustration and pain had become too much. The young people of Baltimore unleashed their anger while America watched: some shocked, some terrified, some righteous and angry. Many others not condoning, but not surprised.

The reasons for this conflict are deep-seated and complex and impossible to disentangle from a history of subjugation and persistent inequality in housing, education, and economic opportunity that puts people down—and keeps them down. But at root those reflexes that allow police officers to shoot down a fleeing man, to abuse him while he's in your care, to assume without confirmation that a black man is "up to no good"—at root this is about a failure of empathy. Failure of connection. Failure of recognizing in one another a common humanity worthy of dignity, support, and respect.

That's why we write. The authors of this collection—all youth of color, many who bear the weight of growing up too fast—are the same youth who could be victims of someone's misguided snap judgment, and it puts their lives in danger. Not only in physical danger—though that risk is

"If our society really wanted to solve the problem, we could; it's just that it would require everybody saying, 'This is important; this is significant.' And, that we don't just pay attention to these communities when a CVS burns, and we don't just pay attention when a young man gets shot or has his spine snapped, but we're paying attention all the time because we consider those kids our kids."

—President Obama

real for these writers—but in the all-too-common psychological danger of having their ambitions derailed. There is a quiet, painful violence endemic to growing up without necessary supports, and it's not about guns and riots. It's about everyday struggle, and the incredible odds we stack against young people who want more, who deserve so much more.

Meet these young people. Listen to them tell their stories—of gratitude, of aspirations for their future, of daily heroism and determination—and hear them proclaim: We Do Not Fit Your Description. We are not victims. We are not thugs. We are big sisters, and sports stars, and academic strivers, and role models. We are powerful, and we are vulnerable. We are your children. See us for who we are. Do something that recognizes: Our Lives Matter.

—Kathy Crutcher
Editor, Shout Mouse Press

SEEN
Tajuan Boomer

Spelling out words to relieve feeling
Shouting out, but nobody's listening

Shrugging shoulder, and rolling eyes
Looking down on ourselves making up lies

Making faces and whispering in ears
Shouting out rumors and facing fears

Beginning 'til the end, it's not fair
Corner around corner, someone's always there

Sitting in the back with folded arms
Hoping nobody sees you to cause any harm

Putting you on blast, making a scene
All fingers are pointing: you have been
Seen.

TAJUAN BOOMER
I am in the eleventh grade and I attend Ballou Senior High School. I am in in AVID and the Teen Outreach Program. I wrote this piece because I feel as though people don't see the real me and what I have to offer. I plan to attend college in the fall of 2016.

WHY I DREAM BIG DREAMS

Aijah Roberts

Because

I want to be a good influence to my baby brother. He's one. He doesn't have a dad. His dad died when my mom was four months pregnant. But that's not what this is about.

This is about my baby brother, and his name is Tony. We call him TJ. J is for Junior. He's attached to me. When I'm dancing in my room practicing for band, he wants me to pick him up. I spin, and he runs to me and reaches up. He's chubby and short and he's got big brown eyes. He doesn't stop playing. He runs around a lot, and he dances, too.

I want him to have confidence, and to be able to do stuff on his own. I want him to play sports, and to feel undefeated. I want him to see how I can achieve my dreams and then be inspired to achieve his own.

Because

I could be the first of my parent's children to go to college.

My parents didn't get a chance to go to college. Instead, I came along. All their money, they spent on me. They had to find jobs in order to support me and themselves. Since they had a lot of

*I've worked
too hard to
give up now.*

AIJAH ROBERTS

I am a 10th grader and grew up in DC. I am a band dancer for Ballou Senior High School. I dream big dreams for myself and plan on going to college. Sometimes I write poems for fun. Writing this piece was a good opportunity to tell people that it's good to try.

Because
I've worked too hard to give up now.

There have been times when I felt stuck. I needed people to push me. It was hard to stay focused because I can get easily distracted. Once people put me down I always gave up. But sometimes you have to ignore the negativity and think about the positive. Now I think of my future. In school, I try to get everything done, to be more responsible. I ask for help when needed and manage my time. I push myself most in English, my favorite subject. I know it's important for my studies, and I understand it. I like my English teachers. The way they teach, they have a method that shows that anything is possible.

I never took anything this serious before. I know I'm getting older, and it's almost time for college, and for me to be an adult. I have to take more responsibility in what I do. If there are bumps in the road, I will simply hop over them. I have a destination.

Because
I dream big dreams not just for me, but for other teens like me, born and raised in DC. I want them to know that you can do it if you put your mind to it. You can be an inspiration to another person like you. You might help somebody do what they love.

Teens in DC have a bad reputation. People think that they won't be anything in life. That they aren't smart. That they won't accomplish anything. But they all have dreams, too. And just like me, they need an open door to walk through.

They need a little brother, like TJ, who makes them feel loved. They need inspiration to push themselves. They need support so they don't give up. And they need someone to believe in them. Everyone needs someone to believe in them.

responsibility, it was hard to pursue their education. So now I choose to finish their footsteps.

I want to go to college because it's important to my mom, and I know she would love for me to live the life she didn't have. I want that life, too. I want to show people that I'm determined. I want to be able to get any job I want. Going to college can help with my professional goals, and with my dancing career. It can show that you can really do what you love. It can help me find who I want to be.

3

*No one
wants to live
in a world
full of hatred.*

DIFFERENT VIEWS, SAME GOAL

Anthony Simpson

In eighth grade, I was kind of problematic. I used to get in trouble a lot. I used to go out and hang out with friends, walking random places, and not get home until 11:00 or later. I was doing okay in school but I wasn't doing as well as I could because I didn't care too much. I have anger problems because I keep a lot of stuff to myself, and so I get irritated very fast. If something is irritating me, I lash out. In the past, when I got mad, I would break whatever was in range, like a closet door, or I might bend a metal pole, or rip clothes.

My friend Maurice's father was a Muslim, so Maurice had always known about Islam. In seventh grade, he became a Muslim, too. We would have conversations about it, and he would talk about how it made him feel happy and jovial. At first, I didn't give it too much thought, but when I was in ninth grade, my mother started going to classes at a mosque in Capital Heights, and she asked if I wanted to go, too. I decided I should.

The first time I went, I felt welcomed. People talked to me like they knew me all their life. Anyone there, it didn't matter who it was. I started going to the classes more often, every weekend. I made it my priority to get up and go. I came to the realization that I didn't have to be so isolated, and people are there for my best interest. That made me feel good as a person, knowing I could go somewhere and feel welcomed, that I could talk to anyone about anything and they wouldn't judge me.

Islam made me feel relaxed and calm. If I was to get mad, I would stop and listen to chapters of the Quran on my phone and read it at the same time. That would relax me. It would tell me that I don't have to be angry, I don't have to be upset. It's been years since I've been in an altercation, not since ninth grade.

Being Muslim helped me be more disciplined, too. I had new responsibilities. I had to practice religion at all times. It helped me organize myself overall. Like in school, I would turn in my work on time, and I started going to class. My grades went up, and I went from having to go to summer school to passing, without needing summer school at all.

But not everyone thinks of Islam as being this force for good in people's lives. Mainstream media in this country often looks at Muslims like we're not people. There used to be a show on TV called "All-American Muslims," but it was canceled because there was an influential organization that called it "propaganda that riskily hides the Islamic agenda's clear and present danger to American liberties and traditional values." All the show was doing was demonstrating how Muslims are just like typical American citizens: getting married, going to school, going to football practice. And yet this group—which vows to "Defend American Values"—managed to get it canceled, and they got Lowe's and other sponsors to drop their funding, too.

But that's just one example, and there are many more. In the Israeli-Palestine conflict, if you do the research, you will see that Palestinians were stripped of their land and forced out or killed off, but much of the media here is making it seem like Jews are the only victims. And there's been a lot of things happening this past year. The same week of the shooting of three Muslim students at the University of North Carolina, someone burned down a mosque in Houston, Texas, and the news barely covered it. At least not the way it should have been covered. Not the way it would have been covered if it was a church.

All I'm saying is even though we have different views, we all have the same goal. Peace. No one wants to live in a world full of hatred. And we don't have to. There are good ways to go about dealing with differences and bad ways. In my life, I've seen both. Let me elaborate by telling two stories.

Story One: Just yesterday, I was at work, and three Jewish young men came in my line. I'm a cashier. They were speaking English like everyone else. And then when they noticed my kufi, they stopped talking, and became silent. Then they started speaking in Hebrew. They were staring at me. When I glanced at them, they looked away. When I rang them up, every question I asked, they aggressively said *No*. It was strange. They were rude, and there was no need to be.

Story Two: One of my more frequent customers is also Jewish. He's cool. You can tell he keeps to himself, but if you open up to him, he'll really talk, and now he comes to my line all the time. One day, after it snowed, it was cold, and he came to my store. I wasn't on a register that day, but he walked right up to me.

The first thing he said was, "Can I ask you a question about religion?"
I said, "Of course."
Then he laughed and said, "I don't mean to sound rude or anything, but does your kufi keep your head warm?"
I laughed, too. "No, not really," I said. All depending on the weather."
"Well I'm Jewish," he said, "and my yamukah doesn't either."

In the first situation there was no conversation. Instead there was tension, caused by our differences. But in the second, there was actual dialogue. There was curiosity and respect. And because of that, there was laughter. We could connect rather than judge.

All I'm saying is, Muslims are people, too. So let's treat each other like we know that's true.

ANTHONY SIMPSON

I am a Jamaican and Cuban Muslim who just wants to give people hope or a sense of pride. I want to be a sportscaster, the first sportscaster on national TV with a kufi on his head. I want to break the barrier for Muslims in America.

HELP WANTED

Brandon Scott

It was a cold autumn night. My face was tucked into my ski jacket because the wind was unbearably chilly. I was sitting at Rhode Island Avenue Station awaiting the next train to take me to Gallery Place. It was going to be my first live NBA game. I always dreamed of going to a NBA game. Nothing in the world was going to deter me from going to this game, or so I thought.

The next train would arrive in twenty minutes. Only one platform was operating due to recent construction on the other platform. I rocked back and forth trying to capture all the body heat that I could.

The train finally arrived what felt like a decade later. I stepped on the train and started towards Gallery Place. It was a long quiet ride. I heard a voice say, "Next stop, Gallery Place-Chinatown," and I stood up and grabbed the rail by the door When the door opened, I did not hesitate to step out. I walked briskly towards to main exit.

As I came around the corner, I heard a loud male voice. It was a tall older guy, late forties or early fifties. He was light-skinned, and he stood with an arch in his back. He also had one of those canes that straps to his arm. He was reaching out to people trying to get their attention, but one by one people just walked past.

I tried to keep my head down and walk pass on the incognito, but I couldn't help

it—I had to look back. He was yelling, "Can someone help me? You? You?" He looked right at me. There was no way to play it off as if we did not make eye contact.

I slowly walked towards him. He started to talk loudly even though I was right in front of him. I looked up at the clock. The game was getting ready to start in less than an hour. I really did not have time to talk to this strange man.

He said something about the elevator being blocked off, and he needed to get to ground level. I looked at the long flight of stairs and knew he couldn't make it. I told him maybe it would be best if he got back on the train to another stop, and got off there. He refused to listen to me and kept explaining the elevator situation.

After a while, he grabbed my arm. He caught me off-guard. I had just moved to DC from West Virginia the year before, and my mother told me to defend myself against any stranger that put his hands on me. I thought it was an act of aggression, but seeing how old and disabled he was, I decided I wasn't going to think anything of it.

I asked if he minded if I stepped away for a minute while I called my sister. She was upstairs in front of the Verizon Center waiting for me. When I called, I explained that it would take me a minute to get upstairs. After a short conversation, she hung up.

When I turned around, the strange guy was still talking to me. As people walked past, they stared at both of us. He seemed like a stereotype, because he looked like a homeless person, and so other people felt less inclined to help him. Knowing homeless people in my family, I knew how he felt, so I knew that I had to help him. Even so, I felt an overwhelming feeling of embarrassment. "What made me agree to help this guy?" I asked myself.

The start of the game was drawing closer and closer. I started to panic slightly. I didn't want to miss a minute of the game.

There was no way he was getting upstairs because of his disability, and the elevator was broken. I came to the conclusion that the best way to get him up there would be to ride the red line train to Union Station because it was just a few blocks away. He could take a taxi to Gallery Place from there. He agreed and we were on our way.

The train came, and we hurried on it. I still had about thirty-five minutes before the game. I was rushing at this point. On the ride he asked me about my name. I looked out the window as if he said nothing. At this point I still felt upset that I was being dragged away from the basketball game.

It took no time to get Union Station. I walked him toward the exit but he said he didn't know how to get to the front from the side exit. I was frustrated by his constant need for assistance, but it wasn't his fault that he needed help. I was just upset that I was running late for the game. I reluctantly offered to walk with him to the main entrance. He smiled. We slowly made our way across the crowded station. I felt eyes laying over my shoulders as I guided this man across the big open floor. That overcoming feeling of embarrassment sat in my chest again.

As we went through both sets of doors, he took a deep breath, nodded his head, and thanked me. At that moment, the feeling of embarrassment turned into a feeling of joy. To know that I helped someone at a time when I really didn't want to was a really important moment to me. It showed me I could help people even at times when I feel like I'm not inclined to help. Sometimes that's when helping helps you both.

When people see me, they do not expect me to be a light-hearted person. They think I'm just another rude, bashful, ghetto kid from Southeast DC who was not "properly" home-trained. That's not the case for most of us. Some of the best people that I know grew up under-privileged like me. We know how the struggle is, so we help others we see struggling. We are a strong community that is often poorly portrayed by people that haven't felt our struggles. How can

someone pass an elderly person and not help him? Was it because he looked homeless, or had a disability? Was it because he was black? All lives—black, white, old, young, typical or totally different—matter. My mother always told me, "Brandon, you can't help everybody, but you damn sure can help somebody." Looking back at what I did that day gives me reason to believe that I did my mother proud.

BRANDON SCOTT

I grew up in West Virginia. I moved to Washington, DC in high school because I wanted to graduate from the same school as my mother. I am highly active. I play a lot of sports, but my favorite is baseball. I am a Christian. I feel that we all have a big impact on how the world operates. One little action can make a BIG difference.

Sometimes helping helps you both.

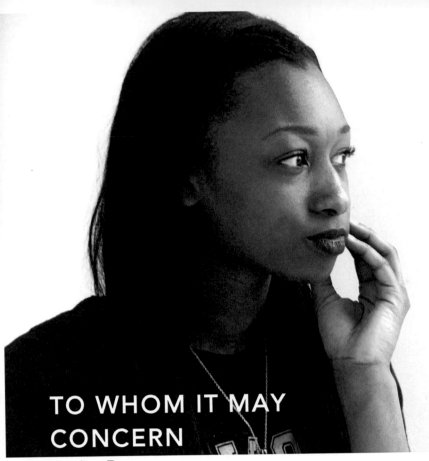

TO WHOM IT MAY CONCERN

Amira Bean

Dear Dr. King,
You had a dream, but
As racists continue to mislead our brains
The thought of fighting back
Is replaced with chains,
And I feel unsafe.

You had a dream, but
As I see it, we're making fools of ourselves
Killing one another
Closing your eyes and once you open them
You still feel like you're being beaten by a slave-master.
And I feel lost.

You had a dream, but
It's time to make it happen!
We need a leader other than the president.
Teenagers, single moms, single dads
It doesn't matter.

You had a dream, but
A call for help is needed.
I'm getting tired of seeing mamas cry.
I'm getting tired of seeing fathers die.

I want change.

See if we don't make a change,
Then the game remains the same
And another R.I.P. shirt is created.

You had a dream—
With strong, well-being young men & women
Of all shapes & sizes—but
I want change.
Change from the skunk of the earth
To making something of myself,
Becoming successful.

So Hey, Dear Everybody,
We need more Dr. King's, Rosa Parks, Malcolm X's.
We need YOU, comrades,
To be the difference in your community
Just by being a better person,
respectful, honest, encouraging.
Make a difference
To be the positive change
To create a legacy
To pass on to the next generation and the next.
They'll follow behind, just watch.

And now I feel…
Rejuvenated.

AMIRA BEAN

I was born and raised in Southeast DC. I am a Senior and Class Vice President, very active in several sports at my school, and working hard to get my high school diploma. I'm headed on to college at University of Maryland Eastern Shore in Fall 2015. I want to major in psychology and become a psychologist. I want to help people cope with their problems. I want to help them become better people.

CARL BROWN

I am now 16 years old. I am a very outgoing, open-minded person, and I love to play sports and travel. I love writing and using what I know to make people proud. I view life and the world from a different perspective from everyone else.

I want to view the world in a whole new spectacular way.

ALL THAT MATTERS
Carl Brown

You think that I am weak, but I am strong.
You think that I bruise easily, you think
that I will fall,
But I tell you, I will stand tall.
You think just because I am different that I
can't make one.
Who are you to judge me.

Some people may think that I am weak because I am different. I don't know the things they know, I don't do the things they do. I don't disrupt, I don't steal, I don't treat other people like THEIR lives don't matter, because that's not true. I'm not them. Yes I live "in the hood", yes I am from Southeast DC, yes I go to Ballou Senior High School. So what. Why do you care where I come from and where I'm at? You should be worried about what I'm made of and what I can do, because I have dreams. I am a caring person and a great friend if you get to know me.

Some people think just because I am where they are that I should be like them.

I have many friends who grew up with me in Southeast DC, and many of them fail to try their best in life and to be their best selves. They do what other people in my neighborhood do. They fight, they hurt people, they smoke, do drugs, and they are rude.

They don't realize the choices they are making. They don't know how much better their lives could be. They don't try hard enough, as hard as I am trying. Maybe they just don't want a change as bad as I do. I feel sorry for them because they may not have the strength that I have to be a leader and not a follower.

The reason I am so different is because I want better for myself. I want to make my life matter. I want to do something no one has ever done, something different and "me." I want to have a career, and an enjoyable one, too. I don't know what exactly yet, but I want it to involve a lot of travel and life experience. I want to learn about the world. I want to go to China and try their food and celebrate Chinese New Year, I want to go to Japan and see the cherry blossoms and bright lights, I want to travel to waterfalls and rainforests, I want to see the Northern Lights, I want to go into beautiful, gem-filled caverns, I want to view the world in a whole new spectacular way. I want to go everywhere possible because life is short. I want to see and do as much as I can.

What I'm doing now to make sure I will achieve this goal is staying in school and staying out of trouble. I get involved with activities and opportunities such as this one—Ballou Story Project—and I do my best. I am looking forward to the future and what it may bring because of the decisions I have made and continue to make. Would you really want to put all of these dreams down just because I am different, because I have a different background, because you think that my life—that I—don't matter?

Who knows. Maybe one day we will come across each other on the street and I could be your boss or your doctor. I could teach your children. I could write the book that inspires you. I could save you with my knowledge, or my skills, or my words. Would you think that I mattered then?

SHUT DOWN

Ayonna Williams

My father Steventh Williams is the person who gives me the most support and advice in my life, but only to a certain extent, because he's locked up. He's been in and out of prison all my life. I haven't spent a lot of time with him in person, but we do write letters.

Close to the end of last school year, he helped me overcome a lot of things at once. He wrote me a letter apologizing for all the time he missed out in my life, and wishing the best for me. He also asked me how everything was going. I told him that family, school, friends, the basketball team, and myself were all stressing. I felt like giving up, but all I needed was for somebody to turn to that would actually listen without asking for nothing in return but a response. He was the only one really there for me, alongside a couple others, but I didn't feel comfortable expressing myself person-to-person at the time. I thought I'd do better with words, so I wrote it out. I said that school was overwhelming. My basketball team and family didn't feel like a family because everybody was against each other. My friends had their own issues, and I also had other personal problems of my own. I was dealing with everything at once. I felt like I was the solution, but I didn't know how to approach it.

Because of everything that was happening, I changed quickly, and it was noticeable enough for others to see that something was going on. The ones who noticed my drastic change asked was I all right but I just said *yeah* most of the time because they were usually the ones who wanted a favor and expected someone to give them something, like everybody owed them the world.

My father was different. He didn't expect anything from me. He told me everything was going to be fine, you just need to take your time and it all will work out. Those were his exact words but in more detail in the letter. He basically told me there are going to be moments in life when you feel worthless and people just want you down, or when there's so much going on that you feel you can't handle it, but you can, you just don't know how yet. He also explained to me that I can't fault myself or beat myself up because of other people's actions even though it's affecting me.

For a little while after that, I shut down. Every day until I went to sleep, I thought about everything he said. It made me look at everything in someone else's perspective. That taught me that another person's point of view is just as important as mine. From that day I realized that I've changed. I speak differently, think about everything I say before I speak. And I contribute, not always looking to help myself, because someone else might need me more than I do. I went to him for advice because I know I needed to learn life lessons that he should have taught me. I have other people I could turn to, like my best friend, who graduated last year, and I'm grateful for her. But in the end, I'm most grateful for my relationship with my dad, and I am going to make him proud.

*I felt like
I was the solution.*

AYONNA WILLIAMS

I'm from Southeast DC. I've been playing basketball my whole life and want to continue my journey in college. My inspiration is LeBron James. I plan on going to a four-year university and double-majoring in math and sports management. It's challenging for me to communicate about personal issues, but I'm overcoming that fear.

ANYTHING IS POSSIBLE

China Warren

I was born in the year 1996, on a Thursday, on the 25th day of April, at 9:25 A.M. It probably was sunny, because it's always sunny on my birthday. Flowers were blooming and birds were chirping, and everything on the outside of the hospital was totally normal. No one knew what was going on inside. They were all living their normal lives, while my life—more extraordinary than ordinary—was just beginning.

I was born twenty-six weeks before my predicted birthdate. When I was delivered by Cesarean-Section I first weighed one pound, thirteen ounces and then later I dropped to one pound, ten ounces. I couldn't breathe on my own because I was underdeveloped and under-oxygenated. Because of this I was announced as a premature infant and was placed in the ICU (Intensive Care Unit) where I lived in an incubator for three months. My teenage mother didn't really know what was going on. She didn't know if she should be worried or scared. She didn't know if I would live or die.

Then they broke the news to her: I was diagnosed with cerebral palsy.

Cerebral palsy is a disability that affects one's muscles, posture, and movement. It can also impair speech. It is caused by an immature/developing brain before birth, some cases happen to be more severe than others. Although it's unfortunate that I have the disability, it is fortunate that my case is only mild. Many people that have a severe case cannot walk which results in them having to be bound to a wheelchair. Luckily for me that is not the case: I can't walk long distances, but I can walk. My disability affects my mobility, movement, and posture, but it is only noticeable on my left side; everything works just fine on the right side.

When I was younger, I was very insecure about my disability. I couldn't do everything everyone else did, and I was too young to understand why not. People would stare, mock, and tease me and sometimes I would hear people whisper things like, "What's wrong with her?" or

I never gave up on myself.

"Why does she walk like that?" It was like I was a circus act in the spotlight.

As I got older, I started to become more aware of what my disability actually was and what it meant, and it was at this time when I became more confident in myself. I was lucky enough to have a strong support system. If I was feeling down, my mom would talk to me and explain why I couldn't do the things that others could, and my grandmother would tell me that it could be worse. Other people deal with worse things than this, she said, and you should feel lucky rather than unfortunate. They didn't want me to pity myself. And I don't want that either.

The doctors told me that I wouldn't be able to walk, talk, see, or do many other essential things in life. After countless agonizing surgeries and therapy sessions, I was able to prove that prediction to be incorrect. My body gave a big "Screw you!" to the non-believers. Now, I'm in the top 10 in my class ranking. I'm in AP classes. I wrote an award-nominated play and an award-winning essay, recently published in the *Washington Informer*. I won one thousand dollars. I am an aspiring author, creator, and dreamer, and there is no limitation to what I can do with my passion for expressing myself. Soon I will be enrolled in college, expanding my intellect and my view on the world. I never gave up on myself. Ever since I was born I made sure I was my own leader.

That is why I strongly believe that anything is possible. The word impossible itself says it: "I'm possible."

CHINA WARREN

I am an 18-year-old female and I am living with a common disability that is called Cerebral Palsy. I have had my disability ever since the day that I was born. I am currently a senior at Ballou and I plan to graduate in June. I love to write and read and I would love to write my very own book someday.

Walk in our shoes.

CHRISTOPHER ALLEN

My name is Christopher. I live in Southeast DC. I'm in the band and I play the tuba, also called the Sousaphone. I'm also a Reach tutor. We go to Simon Elementary School and tutor 2nd and 3rd graders. This is my second year in Ballou Story Project. I came back because it was fun.

YOU THINK YOU KNOW US
Christopher Allen

You think you know why we do things.

You talk all about how we act. You say we don't have home training or manners. You group us like we are all bad, but there are a few of us who have sense of what to do in the world. It's only a certain few who actually don't care about their actions.

You think you know why we sell drugs. You say it's gang-related, that it's crime. The truth is most are trying to help out with our families. And we're too young to get a job.

You say we are liars, we are lazy. You only focus on the bad side that comes out of us. But these are just stereotypes out in the world. Society puts us down, and you don't have the courage to change it.

You say we don't care about anybody but ourselves. You know, everybody may not show they love their mother, but actually, they love their mother. Some people, it's just hard to show their soft side.

What about you. Do you care about us?

Police don't care. Police are supposed to protect the people, and never deny a citizen his rights. But I feel I always have to prove something with police. You can't tell them what you're doing without them running a background check or trying to tag you. It's how policeman see young black men—they simply look at you a different way. You're a young black male, you're doing something bad. That's their first instinct. It makes you evaluate who you can really trust and talk to.

Even some teachers don't care. I heard that a teacher at my cousin's school said, "We don't care if you learn something or not, we still gettin' paid either way." I don't feel that way about teachers at Ballou. They care, they just have a lot of obligations to fulfill, so sometimes they can't focus on just you. They try. But I've seen when there are two or three students disrespecting, and the teacher gets sidetracked and doesn't finish the lesson and says, "Forget it, y'all can do what you want." I know it's hard, but they still have the rest of the class to teach. And we want to learn.

Wanna know what I think?

I think there are a few ways that we can solve this problem and here's one: Education. Start programs that look and sound good and make them creative. Give students opportunities to make up their own ideas. Give them responsibility. Students could do projects, and they could pick people from their community to be in that project. It can bring them closer with their families so they can be stronger and be more widespread in their minds. Be open-minded and not close-minded. That's what we need.

Here's another: Walk in our shoes. Actually come to our homes and see what we go through, daily basis. We'll show you what our life is like. You can also take us out and show us what your life is like, too.

And finally:
Ask yourself a question.
You think you know us.
Do you really?

I want to be that hero,
that mom-figure to children
who haven't had that care in their lives.

HERO

De'Azia Lewis

Last year I almost didn't pass tenth grade. It wasn't because I wasn't smart—I had attended many honor roll assemblies. It wasn't because I'm not a hard worker—I had strived hard on assessments, even when I already had a decent score. Instead, it was because of my family's social and financial status. It was because I missed over fifty days of school.

What were you doing those fifty days? you ask. I was at home watching two siblings, aged two and one. I changed diapers, bathed them, made bottles for them, and took them to play outside. My mother had just gotten a new job helping to save girls who had been trafficked. She wanted the job and couldn't afford daycare, so it was up to me to help out while she struggled to take care of us. I am the oldest child, and my mother relies heavily on my support. I am willing to help, even though that meant academically I was failing.

In my mind I was upset that I had to take care of my siblings at the cost of success, but I knew my mom needed the support. I continued to help her and as a result, I missed over fifty days. I struggled to maintain my grades and was told that I may be held back my sophomore year. At that point I had to take a look at what I was doing, so I went to my counselor to ask her what I had to do to make it through. She helped me express my feelings to my mother and to let her know what was happening to me as a result of my helping her out. My mother told me that she would quit her job to stay with the kids so I could bring my grades up.

Thankfully, Ballou developed an action plan for me to make up all the days I had missed and put me on track to be promoted. I was doing tutoring after school, a credit recovery class, and I took a class in summer school. It was a lot, having to worry about two additional classes at once, and to still have to do tutoring. But I stuck to it and now I am where I'm supposed to be, in the eleventh grade, and I am applying to college.

My mother told me I wasn't going to be a failure, and that I had her support. I knew I wanted to pass to the next grade, because I have plans for my future. I want to be a child therapist. I've watched a therapist actually bring kids in where you could see the pain in their face, but the children didn't want to honestly express what was going on in their lives. I want to be that hero, that mom figure to many children who haven't had that care in their lives. I would love to convince an upset child that not only are they not alone, but they can overcome any obstacle like I did, and that someone actually cares.

DE'AZIA LEWIS

My name is De'Azia Lewis. I grew up in Landover, MD, and I attend Ballou Senior High School. I am 17 and a junior. I am on the modeling team here and enjoy music and spending time with my family when not in school. At home, I am the oldest of twelve other siblings, and I used my essay to tell you how I overcame a hard obstacle.

I'M THE GIRL

Darne'sha Walker

Our lives matter. Because
Our lives should always matter.
I don't want to prove them right,
I want to prove them wrong.
I don't want people to think,
"Oh, she not gon' get nowhere"
"She gon' get pregnant before she get out of high school"
"She not gon' make it through"
NO!
I'm the girl who's gonna finish school,
I'm gonna graduate when I'm supposed to,
I'm gonna finish college, scholarship or not.
I'm the girl who already published two books by the age of 15.
I'm the girl who does everything they think she can't.

But it's not easy. Because
I'm the girl who is always laughing and goofing off so no one knows her pain.
I'm the girl with trust issues, always pushing people away.

I'm the girl who is gonna make a difference.

I'm the girl who no one understands
   who's heart-broken
   who gets yelled at for telling people how she feels.
I'm the girl who is scared to love because the people she loves always lie.
I'm the girl who cries at night because she thinks
    No one loves her
    No one shows her
    No one says it enough.
I'm the girl who is getting replaced
I'm the girl who no one listens to because what she says DON'T MATTER

But they're wrong. Because
I'm the girl who is gonna make a difference.

I'm the girl who's creative, with many talents
I'm the girl who draws, writes, sings, and listens to music to express her ache
I'm the girl who treats people well even when they throw shade
I'm the girl who has a big heart with so many holes to fill
I'm the girl who wants people to accept her for who she is
I'm the girl who is going to be successful at everything she does.

And you know what, so are you.

You're the boy who's going to walk across the stage with his diploma
You're the girl who's going to make it without her mother or father
You're the boy who's going to become a doctor or lawyer
You're the girl who's going to be successful in life

Our lives matter. Because
WE are the next generation
and we're going to change the world.

DARNE'SHA WALKER
I was born and raised in Washington, DC. I like writing and I love music. In my future I want to become a journalist and write about things that matter to me and things that are important to the world. It seems that writing is one of my strengths and with writing you can actually speak to people. You can connect to them.

AMBITION IS THE IGNITION

Diantae Roach

When I was six years old I was acting up in school and getting in trouble a lot. My mother signed me up for baseball to help get me in line.

My first day there, I talked to the coach. Because of my height, the coach put me in the outfield. My first attempt to catch the ball failed, and I dropped it. One of the assistant coaches came out to talk to me and cheer me up. He gave me some pointers about keeping my glove open and also words of encouragement.

Thereafter, I loved going to practice. The team environment was so positive that I couldn't wait to get out of school and get on the field. As I've gotten older, baseball has always been my ticket out of a lot of things, including trouble, stress or even just to have fun and clear my head. In addition to school and baseball, I'm responsible for my two little sisters. I have to help them with their homework, get their uniforms ready, and get them ready for bed. So I always have a lot on my mind.

Every day I see a lot of grown men outside doing nothing with their lives. I guess they had a future, but they ruined it. I always think, "Why can't young black males be a positive influence on even younger black males?" I'd like for us to have careers, life goals, instead of just getting money in the wrong ways. I want to see people getting money by going to work every day rather than people selling weed because they don't want to get a job. I made the decision when I was eleven that I wasn't going to do that. I saw that it wasn't worth it. I don't want to disappoint my mom, to the point where she says, "Where did I go wrong?" I want her to see me when I'm 26 or 27 and say, "I did a heck of a job."

People categorize me. I could be walking down the street with headphones and people will think I'm a gangster. They see me as a thug. But sometimes we're young black men who want to do something with our lives. This one time this white lady called me a gangster because of the music I was listening to. Little did she know I play baseball and I'm on the honor roll. You don't know me, so you don't know who I am.

Sometimes the stress feels like a pound of bricks on my shoulders.

But when I go to the baseball field, it's like…whoosh! Everything disappears and I just have the game to think about. I have always tried to be a leader on every team. I knew that if it wasn't my education, baseball was my ticket to a brighter future.

When I go out there I'm this superhero. It's like I really think I can fly when I play baseball. There's a rush of emotion, especially when I go up to bat. That lady that called me a gangster? That anger is about to be taken out on the ball. I get a newfound love of life when I play baseball.

There have been long days and nights of

practice, aches, pains, and injuries. I've had coaches put me down and try to hold my progress back. I competed against a senior to win his position, and I won! I've run sprints on my own 'til 2 a.m., and I've spent my weekends at batting cages. The reason I have four recruitment letters from colleges like the University of Pittsburgh, Morehouse College, West Virginia University, and the University of Toledo is because I worked for it.

The two things that will guide me to success are my education and the game of baseball. School has always been somewhat of a challenge for me, but I always managed to keep myself on the Honor Roll, get good grades, and even get inducted into the National Honors Society my sophomore year of high school. I want to make my mom, dad, step-dad, and everyone else in my family exceptionally proud of me, not just for baseball, but for my academic success as well. I want to influence my siblings to be whatever they want to be in life.

Sometimes people mistake passion and ambition for arrogance. But it takes a lot for me to go above and beyond, against all these odds, and achieve everything I want to achieve. My confidence is going to take me to college and straight to The Major Leagues. Just give me a uniform.

DIANTAE ROACH

Baseball is my life. I enjoy the sport because it's different. Not everybody plays it, and I don't think about anything else when I'm playing baseball. I grew up in the Congress Heights area and my mother has seven kids, my father has three. I feel good about this piece because it gave me a chance to explain why I act the way I act, why I'm the person I am. I'm going to college next year at the University of Toledo, and I want to be a professional baseball player.

Why can't young black males be a positive influence on even younger black males?

25

DIMONTRE DAVIS

I grew up in MD but came to DC in 10th grade. I've been playing football since middle school, and writing was a hidden talent that I didn't really know I had. My favorite artist is Lil' Wayne because some of his music is artistic, and the words he's using you can imagine in your head. That's what I try to do with my poetry. I plan to go to college and study Business Administration and hopefully become a financial advisor. So I won't be a full-time poet, but this will not be my last poem.

Wake up America
I need you to see
the Malcom, Garvey,
and Turner
in me

MARION BARRY

Dimontre Davis

Real Eyes, Realize, Real Lies
and see clearly that our rights aren't civil,
but based on the skin color of individuals.
People look at us different
not knowing what you've been through.

Should you sacrifice to make it right?
Put everything on the line to live a better life?
But if you don't, then who would?
Questions... Questions... Questions
Who are we second-guessing?

Picket signs, marches, lines of segregation
A plot to divide is the evil we're facing.

This generation needs a mind flash
Our visions are still like a body cast
The only thing we know is money, women, and how that iron blast!

Coming together is nowhere in sight,
but my vision is clear
Praying the dream King seen is near

It's only right that we make it work
Tired of designing RIP shirts
Families in fear, no smiles, just tears...
Is this the life y'all dreamed of?
Before you leave your man, you gotta say, "Be safe, brah."

The streets won't have your back,
It's the education we lack
Needing to devote ourselves to change
or be victims of violent relapse

Wake up America
I need you to see
the Malcom, Garvey, and Turner in me

They tried to slander his name
Which is quite contrary
to the positive legacy of
Marion Barry

*My mother makes
me know that
my life matters,
and that
I can do anything
as long as I
put my mind
to it.*

A MOTHER LIKE MINE

Elexus Brown

My mother is the best thing that ever happened to me.

Her name is Erica Brown and she's 44 years old. My mother is a Christian and OH! She love the lord. She loves church, and praising her God, too. She had seven children in her life—five boys and two girls—and most of the time she raised us as a single parent. She did her very best at it, too. She tried as much as she could, and I admired that about her. My mother is a wonderful person. I love her to the best of me.

Right now I am the only child who lives with her, so she does everything she can to make my life nice. She'll break her back trying to take care of me. My three older siblings live on their own, and my three younger siblings live with their dad. Now see, me, I'm the middle child, and I don't really associate with my father. He has never been in my life and I don't think he ever will. I honestly don't want him to either 'cause I don't need him. I been doing fine for sixteen years of life now, so why should he come back and try to help when I'm almost an adult?

My mother was the one who took care of me my whole life. She took care of me when we were down right and POOR. Like when I was a toddler, we were in a shelter. I don't remember anything about it, but my mother told me, and she showed me pictures. When you live in a shelter you have to leave in the morning and be back at a certain time. And during that time we barely had anywhere to go.

My mother and I, we've been through a lot together.

I think the most powerful gift my mother has given me is that she makes me feel special. All the time. She makes me feel wanted, secure, and loved. She keeps me focused, on the straight and narrow. She makes me know that my life matters, and that I can do anything I want as long as I put my mind to it.

A lot of people out here don't have my type of mother, who loves you, nurtures you, makes you feel good about yourself. Who tells you you're beautiful.

And it shows. Those children start to act out—in school, in public, when they're with their friends. They'll be disrespectful to other adults, and curse. The adults will just look, and say, "Them kids don't have no home training. What do their mother teach them? Were they taught to curse, or taught to respect others?" And then those kids they just feel bad, do worse.

Sometimes when you have a mother like mine, others start to get jealous. Basically they find ways to bring you down, to make your self esteem low. They talk about you, bully you, try to pick on you. They pick on you because you don't have materialistic things. That's what most people value. Especially the ones who don't have it all. The ones who don't have home training or guidance, and their mother is on drugs or out in the streets, their father is either in jail or dead. They're the ones who think their lives don't matter.

They feel bad about themselves. They go home to pity and nothing. They start saying they don't care. They don't care about life. They think NOTHING matters. Including them.

All they need is a home to go to where they can actually sit down and laugh with someone who loves them, like I did.

That's why I care so much about my mother, and I'm thankful that she did everything she did for me. She tried her hardest with me. Because I had a mother like that, I have dreams to go to college. I want to be a plastic surgeon. I want to help my mother the same way she helped me. I want to buy her her own home. To make sure she doesn't want or need for nothing. I want my mother to feel loved, nurtured, and good about herself, the way she did for me. I want to tell my mother she's beautiful.

She's the reason I'll be a star.

ELEXUS BROWN

I was born in Virginia, but I grew up in DC. I'm in the 10th grade, and I attend Ballou Senior High School. I like rap music and street rappers. I plan to go to college so that I can be a plastic surgeon. The college I want to attend is North Carolina A&T. This piece for me was kind of difficult to write, but I got through, and now I can't wait for my mother to read it.

MAKING A CHANGE

Gerald McBrayer

When I was younger, I only thought about football. When I played, I was thinking about me in the future. My dream was to become a football player. I had a talent for it, and me and my family would watch games together. I definitely wasn't thinking about archery. Where I live, where I'm from, archery is not something that's open to me.

Where I'm from is Southeast DC. In Southeast DC, people don't do archery. They do football and they do basketball. Some parts of Southeast, like B Street and East Capital, are quiet neighborhoods and there's not a lot of drama on the block. But other places in Southeast, like in front of the Chinese carryout stores, are not really safe, because people do drugs and they gamble. Once something goes wrong, they will try to shoot the person to get their money back. Wherever you go, there isn't a lot of free space like open fields, and you need space to do archery.

People in Southeast maybe don't even know what archery is. I didn't really either. I had played it in a video game once. But in gym class at Ballou High School, I was going to figure it out.

I got invited to archery. I was in gym and an archery teacher came to teach an archery class. When he was going over instructions, I was listening, but some people were taking it like a joke. So he started picking people who were serious about it. He picked nine or ten people, and I was one of them.

When I got this invitation, I was surprised, because I don't get invited to a lot of stuff. I felt proud of myself. It was exciting because like I said, archery seemed like people played in California or somewhere. Not Southeast. But this man took the time to come here and teach us about it, and some people don't take the time to teach us about stuff other people don't think we can do.

First you had to learn the rules of archery. Then you had to go in the gym where they had targets. You had to step up to the cone. You had to pull back the string with your index and middle fingers, aim at the targets, and release the arrow. It's tough to focus, but you've got to focus.

When I do archery, I get to block everything out: people judging me, peer pressure. Sometimes I feel pressure to do the things others do, like skip class or destroy other people's property. And there are other pressures, too. I gotta block out that worry: Am I going to wake up the next morning? Am I going to live to see another day? Anything can happen. Tomorrow is not promised to anybody.

So it's hard to keep focused sometimes, but not when it's just me and the bull's eye. All of that goes out of my mind while I'm aiming my arrow. I just look and pull and hope I hit the target.

Last year in May, the archery class had a competition. I had to go up against another boy who I really wanted to beat because he beat me in basketball. We got five arrows to get the highest score. We went back and forth, and it was pretty even. In his last shot, he pulled the string back wrong and missed the bull's eye. I thought, "This is my chance to win." When I fired my arrow... I didn't hit the bull's eye. BUT I hit the target near the bull's eye, which was worth forty points, and so I won. I felt victorious.

There was another time when I got an invitation to do something I never thought I'd do... to write this book. In fact I wrote part of another book last year, called *How To Grow Up Like Me*. I was very proud of myself. My mom was proud when she found out about it. I didn't tell her at first about the program because I wanted it to be a surprise. When she saw my story printed, she was definitely surprised. People think that people in Southeast don't even read books, and definitely don't write them. I want to tell people that not all Southeast people are like that. Some Southeast people are capable of writing books, too.

Trying archery and writing a book were both new to me. They were things I thought I couldn't do, but now I feel like I am competition. If I can beat someone else at archery or write a book, I can do other things I didn't think I could do, like go to college. I see that college is hard work, and when I was younger, I didn't think I could last there. But now I'm learning how to handle it. When we have to write a paper in college, now I know to just start with brainstorming. With archery, I learned to not get distracted, to keep my mind on what I'm doing. I think these things will help.

Through these experiences, my life changed. I'm a young black teen with dreads who goes to Ballou... and I wrote a book. I won a competition in archery. Some people think people like me can't do these things. They will not believe it. But I proved them wrong. And I'll do it again.

I proved them wrong. And I'll do it again.

GERALD MCBRAYER
I grew up in Southeast DC. I like sports, like basketball and football. My favorite rapper is Montana of 300. I hope to go to Virginia Tech, where I play to play football and continue practicing my archery.

MY VOICE, YOUR VOICE, OUR VOICE

Erica Branch

"Hey Erocc, you are doing a wonderful job, being diligent, making good music. You are my superstar, Erocc," DJ said to me.

I had just finished recording my second hit, "We Gon' Party," at his home studio, and I was excited. His words meant the most to me because he's a DJ and knows what people want to hear. He's a producer who knows what he is doing. I've always known that music was the path I wanted to take. Music has always been my passion and now since that moment I've had the confidence to pursue my dream.

Music takes me to a place that brings me out of my shell. It feels so free will. Ever since I was a little girl music has brought me to a joyful place. It makes me happy because it brings me to peace. I love being creative and having a different style from others. I love to make songs that are internationally inclined. I want people from different cultures, countries, and generations to love my music. I learned from Pharell, who wrote the award-winning song "Happy," that you can get everyone's attention by appealing to positivity. I don't want to make music about violence. I don't want to make music about drugs, cursing, or hate. I want to make music about partying, being happy, and love. Writing lyrics helps me express my feelings. The studio is where I'm perfectly content.

Music also makes me push myself. I'm very serious about what I'm doing with music. I continue to network with people that have connections to more superior people in the industry. To show that I am hard-working and dedicated I continue to write every day, so when the time comes I'll be well-prepared to perform. I want to study music in college, too. I will learn how to make beats and become better at networking. College will make me legit. I will have a music education, which most people don't have in the industry. I will have more to say about myself. It will help me take my career one step further.

Music is my life. It brings me happiness, wealth, and success. Music matters to me because it helps me become more creative. Writing lyrics also helps me overcome a lot when I'm down. Music makes me feel safe. I know that people feel more safe when their voices are heard.

There are other people in the world just like me who cannot explain their feelings because they may be afraid of society. I'm not afraid. I will speak up for them. My music will be their voice.

ERICA BRANCH

I was born on March 3, 1997. I grew up in Washington, DC. I have two sisters and six brothers. I am the oldest of all. I love to write and create music. Writing lyrics is my passion. My favorite artist is Shawn Carter. He came up from nothing and now is a legend. I am inspired by Onika Maraj and one day I plan on achieving my dream of becoming a well-known CEO of a mega music corporation.

I will speak up for them.
My music will be
their voice.

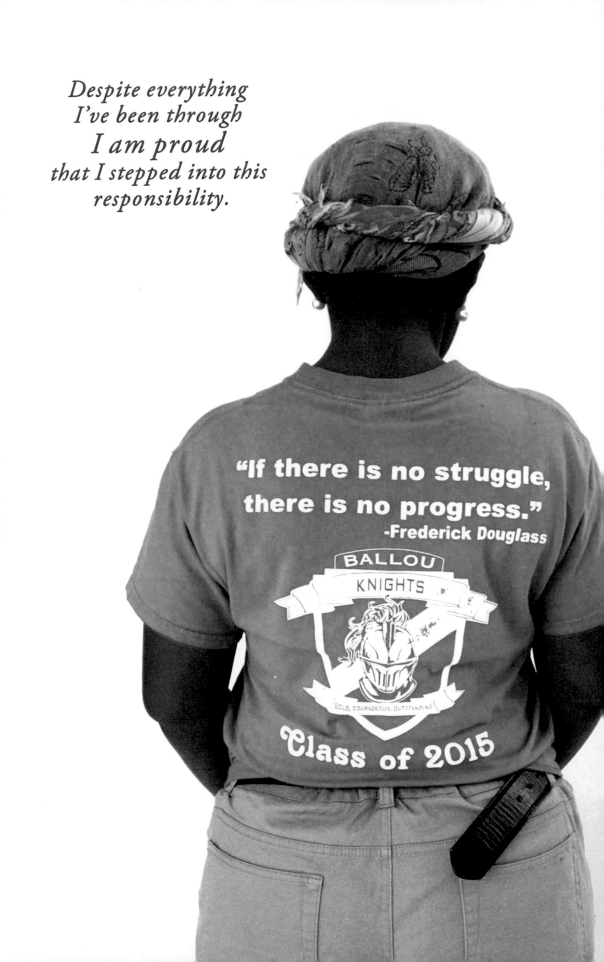

*Despite everything
I've been through
I am proud
that I stepped into this
responsibility.*

ROAD TO ADULTHOOD
K.F.

I never dreamed of becoming a parent at age sixteen. But it's not the way it seems. I didn't get pregnant. I had to raise my sister, on my own.

My mother is currently incarcerated for possession of drug narcotics. When she went to prison, I was left to raise my younger sister who is seven years old. Initially, it was hard because my sister would always ask for my mother and I did not know what to tell her. I also felt helpless because I could not provide shelter for us.

Eventually one of my sisters took us in. However, this arrangement did not last long because she could not afford to take care of us. She put us out, not caring whether we had somewhere to stay or not.

We then moved in with my brother, but after he tried to commit suicide, I had no choice but to pack our clothes and find somewhere else to live because I knew from that day one, it was not a safe environment.

Finally, my oldest sister took us in because she felt sorry for us. As weeks went by I started to notice that every night she had loud music playing, a lot of people over, and she started to use more drugs and alcohol. Seeing this, I realized that if she keeps spending money on drugs, then she won't have money to support my sister and I. I decided that I needed to find a job for more financial support. I got hired with the Teen Outreach Program at my high school as a Peer Educator, where I work every day after school.

Having to raise a 7-year-old is hard on me emotionally because I was forced to grow up and take care of my mother's responsibility at an early age. Sometimes I break down because there are still some things I need to learn about being a woman, but I can't because I have no mother figure in my life. At times I get upset because I can't participate in the activities that I want to because I have a child at home who needs me. There are days that seem harder than others. But, every decision I make affects her life. I face a struggle every day because I know I have to stay focused and continue on the right path so I can be my sister's role model.

Despite everything I have been through I am proud that I stepped into this responsibility to do what I have to do for myself and my little sister. Now I don't see my story as a charity case. I take it as a learning experience. And now I'm a teacher, because I'm sharing it with you.

K.F.
I grew up in Washington DC, Southeast. I like writing poetry and I don't really have spare time. I work, all the time, and I just want to be able to live for myself and not for other people. I'm going to college at Trinity and I'm ready for the challenge. I wrote this piece to use as a personal statement, but when I wrote it, I wasn't too open about sharing. I'm the kind of person who keeps her problems inside. Writing for me is a way to release.

OUR LIVES MATTER

Jermiyah Baker

Sometimes I wanna give up
But I have a lot to live for
We only living to die
So what's really to live for

Where I come from, it's rare we'll make it
And we ain't living for us,
We living for all the rest
The people we intend to satisfy
Her father, his mother, our friends
Portraying to be someone we're not,
Just to keep them pacified

It's just a waste of time,
We alive, but this ain't living
They're supposed to protect us
Instead they're killing us one-by-one
They're supposed to make us safe
So how come it's when they show up
That we get scared?

Why is a stupid question
They get away with it every time
Because it's them, it's not a crime

They have no reason
But there's no consequence
And no chance
For us to live and learn
Making our decisions
Learning from our mistakes
No time for that
Considering

I am black and
They are cops
#BlackLivesMatter

JERMIYAH BAKER

I grew up in Southeast DC. I've got one brother on my mother's side, and on my father's side there's thirteen of us. I like to play basketball and for fun I do anything with sports. This piece was just something that came to mind that describes teens right now. I thought it was important.

*Sometimes
I wanna give up
But I have a lot
to live for*

WHY AREN'T YOU DEAD YET?

Lawrencia Odoms

When I was young I smiled at everything, even the bad things. I was always smiling or laughing at something. Because of this, no one ever knew how unhappy I actually was.

Growing up, I didn't have parents. My mother was heavy into drugs. She was never home, and we barely had food to eat. We ate dry cereal every day. No milk. My father was in prison. He was in my life off and on, but never someone I could count on. That meant I had to take care of my four younger brothers. For a couple years we lived together in a home, and then my grandmother legally adopted us.

My grandmother was amazing at her job, but I was unhappy anyway. The separation from my parents really took a toll on me. Also, I didn't know anyone at school and I was getting bullied. I had to play dumb because when I was smart I was picked on. Throughout those years I contemplated suicide every day because I thought it would be an easy way out.

One day I summoned up the courage to tell my aunt that I was depressed and suicidal. I showed her everything I'd written in the Hello Kitty notebook she had given me a month before. While she was reading I monitored her reaction. She

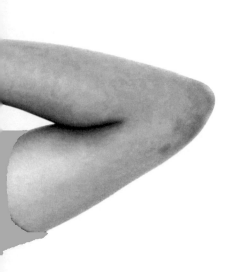

Everyone has a story. Everyone has something to say. And everyone has a life worth living.

I hadn't really thought about why I *didn't* kill myself. When I did think about it, I knew I didn't have the heart to go through with it. I thought of my little brothers. If they didn't have me, they didn't have anyone. And I couldn't abandon them the way my parents did.

So ever since then, I've focused on being happier. I've got friends, my grades have gone up, my brothers are all being taken care of. Mostly I am OK with myself. I know I'm not perfect, and I don't try to be, but I now know who I am. I know that everyone has a story. Everyone has something to say. And everyone has a life worth living.

Sometimes I want to go back to being the person I used to be: the sociopath who never cares. Now I am an actual person with feelings and I do care. I care about life, about school, about love. Though life was easier when I didn't, I'm glad now that I do.

didn't show disgust, but she didn't jump up and hug me, either. Instead she gave me a slight smirk and a raised eyebrow. She asked, "Why aren't you dead yet?"

Shock stretched across my crooked smile. I couldn't answer. Some might say, "Oh my god, why would she ask such a thing?" I honestly don't know why, and I don't know why it hit me so hard, but I'm glad she asked because in many ways I believe that question is the answer to life. Or maybe just my life, because it is the reason I am alive today.

LAWRENCIA ODOMS

I grew up in the DMV. Music is my escape. I know how to play both trombone and trumpet. I've been writing poems and short stories since the sixth grade. I also do photography. Despite my struggles I believe I've had a good life and I wouldn't change a thing about it.

PROVING ALL YOU THINK WRONG

Iyana Ames

My grades prove it.
My knowledge proves it. I know a lot of things.
I know how to solve problems in math and labs in science.
Calculus is my favorite because it's challenging and I like to be challenged.
In biology, I dissected a baby pig.
When you see me, can you see me holding that scalpel?
I saw the baby pig's insides. I touched its heart.

My curiosity proves it.
My risk-taking proves it. I like to experience new things.
I want to go to bungee jumping even though I'm afraid of heights.
I saw it once at an amusement park. There was a bungee cord hooked up and the
woman just dropped. She kept going up and down.
I thought, "That's a long way," but I wanted to do it.
Can you see me there, climbing up that ladder?
Can you see me, screaming loud?

My experience proves it.
My ambitions prove it.
I want to be around more people who are not my color. And not in the DMV.
I went to Paris, France and London, England last spring break. I saw the crown jewels
in London. I went to the top of the Eiffel Tower in Paris.
I met other tourists there, from high schools in California and West Virginia.
They didn't know that in DC public schools we go through metal detectors.
It wasn't shocking to me, but they were shocked.
They were surprised because they didn't experience it like we experience it here.
Can you imagine me, traveling to another country, exploring their differences?
Teaching them about my country? My views?

I never thought I would be able to get on a plane to go to another country.
I never thought that I would even consider bungee jumping.
I never thought that math would be easy for me.

But even though you think that I am dumb
I know I am intelligent
Even though you think that I am afraid
I know I am adventurous
You think I am stuck in Southeast and I'm never going anywhere
And I know I'm well-rounded and curious
All of these are stereotypes of people like me
But I am the only person like me

But I am totally different.

I am the only person like me.

IYANA AMES

I grew up in Southeast Washington, DC. I like to dance and listen to any type of music. My favorite subject is math and science. I plan to go to college to become a pediatrician. This piece was difficult to write, but I wanted to tell you about my life and my dreams.

ON THE FIELD

Levon Livingston

On the field is where I'm happiest. Playing football.
That's where I can be myself.
That's where I can be a leader.
That's where I'm strong, and I am fearless.

On the field, I am filled with so much joy. The joy of being a leader, a team player.

On the field I can be myself while letting go of my emotions. The field is where I live. Ball is life. Without football, I don't know where I'd be.

I haven't always been a leader, and I wasn't always so confident. I never used to talk on the field, or in school, or anywhere. I used to just play. I never knew what to say.

But now, I talk to my team. I give them advice and show them what they need to do. We have a lot of freshman, and somebody had to talk to them. I knew that no one else was going to show them how to be leader, so I stepped up.

On the field it's important to practice what you preach. You work hard, and always give your team everything you have. I give my all on both sides of the ball. You've got to lead by example.

On the field I lead my team through the hardest tasks. After all the battles throughout the game, it's the last moments when leaders step up. Especially when your team is down. Then everybody's putting their head down, and you've got to try to get them to keep their head up. You gotta talk to them, tell them, it ain't over until the clock hits triple zero.

On the field I am strong. I feel like I can push a truck. I enjoy taking out some anger on the man in front of me. I give my all to protect my QB. To do that I make sure I am strong mentally as well as physically. If you loaf, you will be knocked down. You have to have the mindset that you can do anything. You have to believe in yourself and your team.

On the field, we have a lot of fun. Not only that, but we are ourselves. Football builds leadership and teamwork. Football provides structure and improves character. This is why I love the game. This is why it brings out the best in me.

LEVON LIVINGSTON

I grew up in DC with eight brothers and two sisters. We all like sports, but I like and play ALL sports. I plan to go to college and study graphic design. I am going to the University of Kentucky to play football on a full ride, and I am thankful.

On the field it's important to practice what you preach. You work hard, and give your team everything you have. You've got to lead by example.

LETTER FROM THE S2 BUS

M.H. Jordan

Dear People on the Bus,

I was going home in the evening, far from home. I was in Silver Spring, a predominantly white neighborhood, headed back to my home in Anacostia. I had been visiting my mother at college. When I got on the bus I saw a bunch of people dressed in suits and ties. Some of you were listening to music, but some of you were staring at me right in my face.

One of you looked me up and down. You looked sort of disgusted. I was thinking, *Do you know that I can see you?* On my way to my seat, another one of you said to your friend next to you, "Look at how tight her jeans are." I heard mumbling, too, but I don't know if that was about me. I felt uncomfortable, and I was frustrated because we all live together. Why are you all looking at me like we're not the same people?

My first reaction was to disrespect you the way you disrespected me, but my parents always told me, *Don't feed into it, you don't have to have a reaction to everything.*

But if I could, I would ask, "What is the difference between you and me, other than our skin color and what side of the river we're on?" I was thinking, *Sometimes you see women getting on the bus in tight yoga pants. Y'all are judging me, but you're wearing the same things.*

When I went to sit down next to you, lady, you looked scared. Your eyes got big and you sat back and moved out of the way like you were trying to escape. I wasn't going to do anything, I just wanted to get a seat. Maybe you think we all want to rob somebody or get in a fight, but that's not me. That's not all black people. Maybe you don't know black girls like me. When I'm in school, and I write a paper, if someone comes in to observe the class they will say, "Did you write this yourself?" When I'm texting friends my

I define who I am.
I am a proud black child.
I am intelligent.

And regardless
of what surrounds me,
I will push through
to be at the top.

age and I use a big word, or when I use a big word in conversation, they say "I didn't know you knew words like that." They think we're supposed to use only slang and that I am using words that only teachers use at school. But I write essays, and stories, and I read a lot, and I know that's not true. I know how to talk when I'm in a professional environment. I can code-switch, and I know I need to do that so that people like you, lady on the bus, will listen to me.

While I'm sitting there next to you, I get this feeling to tell you everything about me. You need to know: I've brought a whole auditorium to their feet. When I was working with the Ballou Story Project, my essay was entered into a city-wide contest. My piece was a story about my life, and I won third place and $200, out of all the students in DC. When I won I was happy because I doubted myself even being in the top 100. But to know I won something, well third place,

it gave me a very proud feeling, not to mention I'm coming from a school that everybody doubts and always has something negative to say about. While I was on the stage reading, I tried to imagine everyone listening to my story and loving it. And their applause and standing ovation afterwards showed they did. But while I was actually reading, I was terrified. Instead I imagined everyone listening to my story just like, "How did *she* get in third place?" I still have those feelings of doubt in my mind. Maybe because of people like you, lady on the bus.

While I'm sitting next to you, I wonder about your life. I wonder how much you accomplished in your high school career, how your life compares to mine. But I don't say a word to you. And you don't say anything to me. And when we get to my stop I get off and we still don't know anything about each other, except for who's black and who's white.

So now I'm writing to you, People on the Bus, to let you know that all your rude comments, disrespectful looks, and doubts do not define who I am. I define who I am. I am a proud black child. I am intelligent. And regardless of what surrounds me, I will push through to be at the top.

I hope this letter reaches you. And once you read it, I hope you understand.

Sincerely,
M.H. Jordan

M.H. JORDAN
I grew up in Maryland and DC. I am a sophomore at Ballou Senior High School. I like to read and write ... for fun. Writing for the Ballou Story Project isn't hard to do but making it interesting can be. Working on this piece was a good experience that I wouldn't mind doing again.

THREE POWERFUL THINGS

Rickkia Jackson

My grandmother would always say, *What you do in the dark, comes to the light.*

And instead of doing right, I was doing wrong.

I would always be lying. Waking up late for school. Standing in the hallways twenty minutes after class started. Outside of school I was playing basketball, going to friends' houses. Instead of working, I was distracted. I used to skip classes and the school would call my grandma, so I would lie to stop a lot of confusion.

But when I saw that my grades were dropping, I knew things had to change. I knew if my friends were making good grades, I could do the same. Three powerful forces helped me make that change. And I don't know where I'd be without them.

1

My first key to success was my grandmother. She was always there for me, leading me on my road to riches. Grandma always motivated me by telling me how she did not go to college and how I should attend, how it would change my life around. My grandmother told me to always be the leader, not the follower, and to work hard and make good grades. She told me the only way out of poverty is an education, so that inspired me to push myself to raise my GPA to get into the school I want to get into, the University of Maryland. And now here I am, writing a book, on my way.

2

Basketball helped me change because I love sports, and without that, I would be getting into a lot of trouble. Basketball keeps me busy, and it gives me something to do after school instead of fighting for

Nothing is going to be handed to you. You have to work for it. Go get it. You have to want to work hard to become a success.

reasons that were uncalled for. I learned from basketball that hard works pays off. For example, as a power forward I was struggling to shoot free throws. I kept practicing during basketball practice and after school and on my own time in the gym across the street from my house. After three months, my shots improved. There was one time when we played against Maths, and they usually beat us. Three minutes left in the game, the score was 61-58, them. I had the ball and I drew a foul. I went to the line and shot two. I felt a lot of pressure because if I made them there was a chance of us winning. I made them both, and I don't think I would've made them if I hadn't practiced. We ended up losing the game, but I felt proud of myself because I practiced and I made them. After that I felt that I could do anything I put my mind to.

3

Finally, I found the force to change within myself.

I worked myself so much, I knew I could do whatever I put my mind to. I came to class on time and paid attention and all my hard work paid off. My grades were going up. I did my homework to improve my test scores. I stayed after school to get any of the work that I missed during class. I chose to move my seat, which changed a lot in myself. It made me focus instead of talking to my friends. I actually made the learning environment better. I made my friends start to do better because they knew that I wasn't trying to fail a class that I had the potential to pass.

Now I am doing better than I was before. I'm staying out of trouble, learning to go talk to somebody instead of fighting. When somebody is bothering me for no reason, I used to take matters into my own hands and fight them. Now I go to administrators or my parents.

In the next five years, I want to be playing college basketball at Maryland, and then go to school for law, criminal justice. I want to stop gun and domestic violence, because where I grew up, people get killed, and I want everybody to be able to walk out of their house and feel safe.

I would like to thank my grandmother for pushing me and motivating me to do good in school and work hard in life because nothing is going to be handed to you. You have to work for it, go get it. You have to want to work hard to become a success.

RICKKIA JACKSON
I grew up in Washington, DC. I'm 15 years of age, and I'm in 10th grade. I play basketball and flag football for Ballou. My grandmother raised me and I'm thankful to her.

WHAT YOU NEED TO KNOW

N.C. Kitt

You think

that because I live in DC I live in poverty. But I actually have a mother and father and a wonderful roof over my head. The door is red. It's different, it shows that it's my house. No one else's house has a red door. Our neighborhood is clean. It's quiet, it's a one-way street, and there are not a lot of children there. Our street is long, and there are a lot of old people. Good people. I live in Northeast, in the inner city, but it's peaceful and it's different from my school environment. My school's neighborhood has a lot more people. It's loud, and there's more congestion. When I come home from school, I feel peace and serenity.

You think

that because I go to Ballou, I'm not learning anything. But I actually have a 3.8 cum. and I get my goal accomplished. At Ballou, they push you to do your best. And I'm not just learning how to pass my tests. I've also learned harder things, like that you've got to be tough. At this school especially, you can get distracted. All your friends are there, and you've known them for a long time. And your teachers are often absent. They got a lot going on, too. You've got to be prepared for anything that comes your way. And Ballou has taught me that, through the community, the students. I am learning life lessons here, in just the tenth grade.

You think

that because I write, I'm nerdy. But I like writing. I write poetry. It's a different feel, like a release. A personal medication. I write about me, about how I feel about things in school and how I enjoy my days with my friends and family. When you come to school, you have different emotions every day. Some days you're glad to come to school. Sometimes you feel overwhelmed. When I write it down, I don't feel so cluttered. I don't feel that everything I'm stressing about is on my mind. I just write it down, and I feel free.

I think

that everybody should have a method to feel free. And not everybody does, because sometimes they get trapped by what

You think.

I'm not going to let that happen to me. I'm not gonna let the odds defeat me. I'm not proving them right. I'm different. I know my strengths and I that I can overcome. And I'm going to do my best not to let others get trapped either. When I grow up I want to be a therapist, and I'm going to listen to people. I'm going to take notes about what that person feels and figure out how to help them. And the main thing I'm going to tell them is:
Stay Strong.
Focus on You.
And Believe.

N.C. KITT

I'm 15 years of age. I like R&B music and my favorite artist is Jacquees. I plan to go to college and become a family therapist. This piece was not so difficult because these were open thoughts, and I like to write about my thoughts. Writing about my thoughts makes me feel like I don't have to worry about it anymore.

I'm not gonna let the odds defeat me. I'm different. I know my strengths and know that I can overcome.

ALL THE DIFFERENCE

Sad'e Burrell

I believe in the saying "You never know what you have until it's gone." There are lots of reasons why I believe this but one stands out to me the most. Everyone has someone in their life that passes away.

On July 25, 2011 my grandmother had a heart attack and died. During this time I was in a program that was getting me ready for my 9th grade year at Oxon Hill High School. That day I was in the computer lab with people I did and didn't go to middle school with. There were the original Dell computers.

While I was in there I got two calls from my older sister and one call from my father. I didn't pick up because I was busy. I should have answered the phone when I had the chance. So then while I was going home on the yellow school bus, listening to my music, I got another call,

from my mother. I finally picked up on the third ring.

She sounded strange and told me not to get on Facebook. I responded with, "Okay, that was awkward."

When I got off the bus I went to my house on top of a steep hill. My mother wasn't there and neither was my older sister. My three younger siblings were there, but I paid them no mind, so I fell asleep on the couch due to the heat and being exhausted.

My mom woke me up. When I woke up I saw my entire family. They had a look of sorrow on their face with the exception of my younger siblings. They had McDonald's bags in their hands.

Before I could ask, "What's in the bag?"

I want to
inspire people
to be better
than they thought
they could be.

my mom said, "Sit down. We have to tell y'all something." I knew this was not good.

She took a deep breath. "Your grand-mother passed away this morning."

I didn't think. I just said "How?" I instantly thought someone killed her, so I was furious, just staring at the DVD collection we had by the TV.

"She had a heart attack," she said.

At that point I didn't feel anymore. I didn't want anything to eat but I had to eat.

After the bad news I told my boyfriend. We sat on the staircase in my apartment building as it was raining outside. I was crying because my grandmother was my best friend. We did everything together. We played Uno cards, Phase 10, board games, everything. It was that bond that we had. She felt like another mother. She made me be outgoing. She made me joyful.

The day of her funeral I wasn't prepared.

When I saw her lying there in the casket wearing a purple dress with matching earrings and a necklace I automatically began to cry. The tears were non-stop. My grandmother's older sister came in the sanctuary and began to scream and holler at the top of her lungs as if she were being kidnapped. Then my great-grandmother tried to lift my grandmother up and started crying.

Through the entire funeral I was crying and then got a major headache from crying so much. When my cousin Chris and my older sister Jasmine said what they remembered of her I started crying because I could hear her voice, her laugh. I could see her smile, everything. Then my cousin Pinky began to sing "His Eye Is On The Sparrow" by Whitney Houston. More tears.

After the funeral and the gravesite in Quantico, we went to my church, Second Baptist Church, and ate ham, turkey, mac & cheese, collard greens, and pie. It was good, but hard to enjoy anything without my grandmother.

My grandmother showed me how to be happy. She showed me how to make others happy, too. I want to move others the way she moved me. I want to help people if they're shy. I can help them be more outgoing. If people have problems they're going through, I can help them, talk to them, or I could just listen, too. That's part of what people need. Most importantly, I want to inspire people to be better than they thought they could be. My grandma taught me that, and in my eyes that made all the difference.

SAD'E BURRELL
I'm from DC even though I moved around a lot between MD and DC. I like to sing and dance around for fun. My hobby is tennis.

HEARD IN SILENCE

Randy Sams

So the other day, I go to the liquor store and the store owner can't take his eyes off me, like I want to take everything visible. I'm frustrated but try to remain humble. As I keep browsing for a snack, the more I feel tension aimed in my direction.

So I ask, "Why do you keep staring at me?" I'm thinking, *Like I want to take something from this place.*

He says, "Too many kids like you that came to this store. Took away my trust."

I feel so angry that he would say this. I don't even stop to get my snack. I turn to leave and to find someone to understand me.

While I'm walking, I'm furious. I wish that I had stayed. I picture myself having a conversation with this man to figure out why he's got these emotions for "kids like me" who come to his store. This is how I see it in my head:

Me: "Why do you feel this way?"

Him: (*No words. Puzzled face.*)

Me: "Wipe that look off your face! I need to understand why every young black male is a criminal to you."

Him: (*No words. Pretends to check the cash register and count the profits that he had made throughout the day.*)

Me: (*Getting angry.*) "Pay attention to me. You think you know everything but you don't know me."

Him: (*Frustration. Finally he says...*) "*You* think you know everything with your hip clothes and your new slang but you don't. I see your future. You are most likely to be one of them men on the corner asking for a cigarette."

Me: (*Surprise.*) "You don't know what my future holds. You don't know that I will graduate from college with a degree in mechanical engineering. You don't know that I could change this whole community with just one invention. Think about it. You don't know."

It feels exciting to imagine the things I would have said to the man. It would have made me feel like I stood up for myself and my people. I want to have this conversation, to show that I can be more outspoken than most people who come to the store. I want to show him that we all don't solve our anger with violence.

The way this guy treated me makes me want to do something with my life so I can prove them wrong and say, "Who's successful now?" No one in my immediate family went to college. It makes me want to be the first. My mother doesn't see me putting the effort to get into college, but I am. I keep my grades up, focus on doing all my essays. I am in band, playing bass, and I am in Reach, where we help students in second and third grade improve their vocabulary and reading. The things I do help build my community, and I'm breaking the stereotype that black males don't do anything to help or don't have any ambition.

The things I do help build my community, and I'm breaking the stereotype that black males don't have any ambition.

I didn't get to tell him any of this, but I am telling you:

You think that I am a menace to society.
You think because I'm a different color,
because I came from slavery descent,
that I can't make greatness my reality.
You say I can't help the world change for good
But I correct you critics
with the brightness of my future.

RANDY SAMS

I was born and raised in DC, and I love all genres of music. I'm the leading bass drummer in band at school, and that feels both stressful and wonderful. The other thing I'm passionate about is writing poetry. I found my passion for writing in the 8th grade. Sometimes I enjoy playing sports. Otherwise, I like to be out the house and go places.

NEW BEGINNINGS

Shaquon Wells

There was a point in my life when I felt like there was no way that my life could get better. I was eight years old. My family was a normal family who worked hard and always stayed together. We never really got mad at one another or had arguments. We were an athletic family. We all played sports, like I played football on a Boys & Girls Club team. My family—my grandmother, grandfather, aunt, mother, and I—went to church every Sunday. I felt like life was good, like I didn't have to worry about anything.

But something happened during my transition from second to third grade, and I made a big step from being a young playful kid to having to grow up fast.

In second grade, my grandmother was diagnosed with cancer. I couldn't go into her room because my parents didn't want me to see her in that light. My parents told us what was happening, and I saw her start to lose her hair and her teeth. She was getting weak and had to go back and forth to the hospital. I got to see her one last time in Greater Southeast Hospital before she took her last breath.

I knew I had to be strong for him. I was always thinking about how I could better myself.

But it didn't really hit me that she was gone. I was thinking that everything would be okay because I still had my mother, my aunt, and my grandfather.

A couple months later, something happened to my mother. I'm still not sure what happened because my grandfather and aunt won't tell me. One night, me and my little brother were in the living room and she left, like she was going to the car, leaving us alone. A few hours passed and then a neighbor knocked on the door, like a panicked knock, loud and scary. I never had the courage to open the door—something told me not to. Eventually the police and an ambulance came, and when I saw it was the police, I opened the door. The policemen came in and started talking to me, asking if we had any phone numbers of our grandparents or any other family members, but I didn't know any numbers, and my brother was three, too young to understand what he was saying. The police told us to grab everything that was important to us. I grabbed my X-Box, and my little brother grabbed a toy, and we took some clothes to take us through the night.

Around 1:00 a.m., a social service woman came and told us to get in the car with her. We got in, and she said she was taking us to a foster home.

When we were alone in the bedroom of this new place, my little brother started crying and asking why we were there. I couldn't give him an answer. All I could say was that we would be okay and everything would come out right in the end. I knew something bad had happened to my mother because she wouldn't leave us alone in the house that long. I started to think that she might have passed, but I felt like I had to protect my brother. I stayed up the whole night thinking about the situation and what had happened to my mother.

The next day when we woke up in the foster care home, there was another boy there. It seemed like he had a problem with us. He was older, like a teenager. He had a problem with us being in his room. I felt like I had to keep my brother away from him, because I could see that there was something wrong with this boy, so I tried to keep us safe.

While we were in foster care, my little brother and I had to sleep on the floor. We lay there, still not knowing what had happened to our mom. All I remember from being in the foster system was thinking about the police coming in our home and telling us to grab everything important to us. I never questioned anything that the police asked. We did as he said and left our home.

After staying in foster care for a few days we finally got back with our family. We went to our great-aunt's house first, because she was a foster parent. Not long after that, my grandfather and aunt came and we went back with them.

When I got to my grandfather's house, almost my whole family was there. I didn't know what was going on, but that night I received news that would change everything. That night I was told that my mom had passed away. For some reason I did not cry or show emotion. It was like I shut down.

I never forgot what it felt like that night, like all my brother and I had was each other. I knew I had to be strong for him. I was always thinking about how I could better myself. This hard time in my life always kept me strong, and kept me going, to get past any disadvantage that I faced. But still, I struggled. I didn't always do well in school. In ninth grade I didn't have the best grades, and in tenth I tried to get on track, but I couldn't get it right.

Once I came to Ballou, I had the opportunity to do what I knew I could do. Ballou gave me the chance to show that you can come from what you came from and do better in your life. Having to take care of my little brother helped me be a strong leader at Ballou, and everybody on the football team voted for me to be captain. It made me bold, and it made me stand out more in the teachers' eyes. My social studies teacher wrote me an email telling me he had written a recommendation letter for college, and he said, "You certainly represented Ballou well, but you also made me personally proud to be your social studies teacher. Thank you for all your hard work and insight. You are one of a kind." This made me feel good, like I could make an impact not only on myself but on the people around me.

My brother is doing very well now. He's getting good grades in school and he's on the football team, too. Next year, I'm going to Old Dominion University, with a different mindset of how I can make myself better. Instead of having to look after someone else, now I can look after myself.

SHAQUON WELLS

I grew up in Southeast Washington, DC, not really knowing much about the city, but just knowing that I wanted to get out. Football is something that helped me stay grounded, and to know what I can do to be better in a place where nothing really good happens. I am going to study psychology in college so that I can be a therapist. I can see myself being very successful, living the life that I always dreamed of. I'm on my way to new beginnings.

BEING ME
Sharhonda Lewis

Living in Southeast DC ain't easy. You have to face many challenges being a black teen trying to make it out the hood. You have to face peer pressure, gang beef, shootings, killing, people bringing you down, and no one trying to help you up. In this city we call DC it's a blessing to survive.

My experience in DC hasn't been perfect. Some of my days have been high and some of my days, really low.

My mommy became sick when I was only in the 5th grade. In the 5th grade reality did not set in that she was never going to get better. I had the idea that hope was alive and I wouldn't have to live with my granddad and cousin anymore. But at 5th grade graduation everyone else had their parents there. Not me. I really didn't know how to feel, so I cried. I wasn't sure if those was sad tears or tears of joy.

I asked my sisters what was wrong with Mommy, and they always brushed it off, or told me they didn't know. My oldest sister knew, but she wanted to spare my feelings and wouldn't tell me what it was. I still don't really know exactly what is wrong.

What I do know is that my mommy lives in a nursing home. I've visited her twice in seven years. I don't like seeing her like that. The last time I went, I held her hand, and neither of us really talked. She didn't even know who I was.

Many times in middle school I was faced with the question, "Where is your mom?" I felt embarrassed, and sometimes I lashed out at whoever asked. When I started high school, I didn't have many people to lean on, and I had to be my own supporter. I went to Thurgood for my first two years and it was terrible for me. Academically, I struggled. I hadn't had good teachers in middle school, and I couldn't keep up. I had to go to summer school, and for 10th grade I was determined to get out of there.

I wasn't so sure about coming to Ballou, but when I did, I knew it would change my life forever. As a senior, I'm now the Class President of 2015, and with that title comes pressure, so you need determination and discipline. Both things I thought I didn't have. But I wanted to have those things, so I had to make minor changes, like changing my friends. I used to be friends with people who wanted things from me. They'd want money, snacks, things they knew I wouldn't say no to. I realized that when I was down, those friends were never there for me. We had arguments in class and I was switched out of those classes. That turned out to be a blessing because now I'm in classes with people who had my back in the first place.

When I changed my friends I became happier and got to know others, people I never gave a chance to. I got encouragement from my cousins, who told me I was smart and I deserved better than how people were treating me.

As Class President, I've tried to make us closer. I made it so everyone has opinions and a voice. We had a protest to get one of our vice principals to listen to us. It worked because the next week we had a senior meeting with her and our class sponsors. We told her that we felt that our feelings hadn't been addressed. It's not easy to be a leader, and I've cried several times because I felt like I let them down. Deep down inside I know that I cannot make everyone happy.

At times I see myself taking five steps up and then three steps back, though I never do that on purpose. Like one day when I was being selfish and blurted out, "Come help me!" at Ms. Erazo, my AVID teacher, instead of raising my hand. In that moment, I felt suddenly that she thought I wasn't important, and I felt neglected. I sometimes need assurance that I can do things on my own.

I can honestly say I'm not ready to graduate high school. I feel like we needed more time than this. I feel safe here, and I stay here all day. When I'm here I feel at home because people value me. I also feel like the time is coming for one chapter closing and a new one beginning.

All I know is I don't want to be another statistic in DC, ending up pregnant or dead or without a job. I want to be successful and be able to financially take care of myself and my family.

I also know I'm determined to make my mommy proud, even if she doesn't know me. Life is not easy, but I smile each and every day. I show the world that I am brave.

Life is not easy, but I smile each and every day. I show the world that I am brave.

SHARHONDA LEWIS
I am 17 years old and I am the Class President of 2015 at Ballou Senior High School. I am determined to be successful and hope that my story encourage others to speak out.

FIRST HISPANIC GENERATION

Triony Valdivia

In 1998, life in Santa Cruz, Bolivia, was scary. There were shootings, low-paying jobs, and struggles to pay for food and to put a roof over our heads. Hoping for a better life, my parents packed up our family and brought us to the safe haven of the United States. They wanted to give us tools to be safe from the streets, to make connections to other people whom we could trust, and to make our education our priority.

Now I will be the first member of my family to attend college. I've been grateful for the opportunity for education here, but there are always obstacles. One obstacle is the assumptions people have about Hispanics. Some people think we move around a lot, that we have no interest in education. This is a stereotype, because I persevere in my schoolwork even if I recently moved or am about to move to another place.

Another obstacle is that sometimes the schools I've attended have made it difficult to achieve my goals. Especially since I've moved to Washington, DC, I've attended schools in poverty-ridden, crime-infested neighborhoods. The statistics in my neighborhood are depressing: only 56 percent of students graduate from high school according to Emma Brown, a reporter for the *Washington Post*. Many of my peers live with grandparents instead of their parents because they may be incarcerated or separated. Sometimes the grandparents may not be able to be good role models due to the lack of support from their parents. I'm very fortunate: my family is together, and I am determined to go against the trend of low educational achievements that is prevalent in DC's Wards 7 and 8. I am working hard to be valedictorian at Frank W. Ballou Senior High School and will prove that taking advantage of education can lead to success.

During my 11th grade year, I was appointed as an OSSE Scholar, one of the top 60 students in DC, and was chosen to attend college over the summer and live on campus. I was very nervous, but also excited, to attend Syracuse University. I took advantage of this by balancing my academics and social life. I learned that hanging out was very tempting so I studied in the library to avoid distractions and keep on track of achieving a C or above in Law and Engineering. I knew that college work would be difficult so I spent at least two or more hours studying and working on assignments every day. Then I explored the campus by participating in activities and finding nearby stores to buy personal goods and get the feel of being independent. When the program ended we said our goodbyes and promised to keep in contact. After that summer, OSSE inspired me to attend college, not just for the social life, but for what I want to be in the future: a mechanical engineer.

Education is a huge part of my identity. Therefore I will give back every penny that my parents gave me to make them proud and to fulfill their hopes for me. I want to achieve what they once wanted for themselves, because their parents weren't able to give them the support to attend college and earn a degree. My mission is to work hard, become a mechanical engineer, and be successful in life. I'll break down stereotypes about Hispanics and show the world who I really am.

TRIONY VALDIVIA

As a member of a low-income Hispanic family who moved one place after another, I got a fresh start every year. I play soccer and I love it because of the teamwork, exercise, and leadership. I am going to college next year to be a step closer to success. I will break the cycle of going to work after high school. I want to show all Hispanics what is worth doing to be successful in life.

I am working hard and will prove that taking advantage of education can lead to success.

THAT'S DEEP

Tyandra Ames

Many people have made an impact on my life, but one person stands out. My teacher, Ms. Erazo, has changed me in so many ways. She put me on a path I never thought I would take.

I met Ms. Erazo in my ninth grade year. She was so full of energy and always had a smile on her face. She loved snapping her fingers and saying, "Mmmm, that's deep." It felt like I was at home. She became an influential mentor to me.

Before Ms. Erazo, I never knew how important a first impression was, or how you should speak in front of certain people. Ms. Erazo always talked about how character building and code switching are key things to get through life. Coming from middle school I had no clue what those things were. She explained it to me and gave me a better understanding to who I truly was. I called it my training to success. With just the start of me building my character and talking a bit better I was nominated into the National Honor Society. From there, with the help of Ms. Erazo, I joined several leadership groups like AVID, Ballou Youth Leaders in Action, and Honor Roll, and I even became Junior Class President.

But these successes bring lessons, too. There were times when something good happened to me, like winning an honor or awards, and I would brag about it. Ms. Erazo would always tell me, "Don't brag too much, because the switch can flip in a blink of an eye." I never bragged again, not even for the major things.

I've had lots of role models who could help me in life—like my older sister who could tell me things that I needed to get started on the right path—but most couldn't really understand who I truly was. I'm like an onion: you have to peel me back layer by layer. Ms. Erazo knew the only way to get to my core was to use a knife. That's how it's been since my ninth grade year. She could always read me. She once told me that "It's not about who's right or wrong, it's about how you heal." I still think about this saying, and it has helped me through a lot of challenges.

There were times when I doubted myself, thinking that I would never be perfect, or that I didn't matter. Time and time again I would fail, and sometimes greatly. It would get to a point when I gave up on everything, even myself. I didn't know how to bounce back from a "great mistake." I had never made as many mistakes as I have now. It's been a big change since middle school. But Ms. Erazo always reminds me that "the only way to improve is to make a mistake." She also tells me, "Never tell yourself that you don't matter, because once you do, people will treat you like you don't matter." With these words I knew that I had the power to control myself and to make good choices. With the help from Ms. Erazo, I built my self-esteem back up. I became more of an advocate for myself, and for students at my school. She allowed me to tell other people they matter, too.

Ms. Erazo makes me think about the future. She talks to me not just about going to college but about pursuing a career. When I get older I would like to become an international criminal lawyer.

At first I gave up on the idea and wanted to go the military or become a teacher. But Ms. Erazo told me to keep my head up, and that I had big dreams that can take me far.

Without Ms. Erazo I would have a really stressful life. To me she is my personal therapist. She helps me through everyday life and everyday problems. I can go to her about anything. I'm glad that I decided to come to Ballou my ninth grade year so I could meet Miss Erazo. She changed my high school thoughts—and my life—all the way around.

It's not about who's right or wrong, it's about how you heal.

TYANDRA AMES

I have six sisters and four brothers and I live with my mom and dad. I am the Junior Class President. I am a part of the Ballou Majestic Marching Knights Band as a Royal Dame. My dream college would be to go to Yale University for my J.D. degree to become an International Criminal Lawyer. I enjoy dancing, singing, reading, and joining various groups at my school.

AFTERWORD

My students are incredible people. They may come from the same community, but each one is unique and their stories are powerful. It is my deep desire that by reading this book, you will have the opportunity to see a kaleidoscope of color, experiences, and stories—each one giving you just a degree of difference into who my students are, where they come from, and more importantly, where they are going.

As beautiful as that may sound, however, the truth is that my students often have experiences that confirm what society tells them to be true about themselves, which is that their lives matter in theory, but not in practice. Their lives matter when it's convenient, but not at all costs. It's hard for them to believe that all people are equal, when they often feel targeted just because of the color of their skin.

But they're not letting society's perception of them stop them from dreaming, stop them from reaching, stop them from living with purpose. Their lives do matter because they choose not to be passengers in this ride of life—they choose to take charge and become something beautiful, despite the brokenness that we all experience as humans in a fallen world.

May their stories echo in your hearts. May their experiences cause you to reflect. And may their voices be heard all throughout DC and across the country because their lives matter. Not just to me or to each other, but to their community and, ultimately, to the world.

—*Shajena Erazo*
Ballou High School Teacher

ACKNOWLEDGMENTS

The Ballou Story Project could not have been possible without the support of a number of hard-working folks who believed in the importance of empowering these young people to share their stories.

For coordinating these writers every week, we cannot thank enough Ballou teacher Shajena Erazo. Ms. Erazo was the motivating force behind these authors, and she gave selflessly of her time over and over again to make this project happen. She is an inspiration to her students and to those of us at Shout Mouse Press.

For mentoring these writers each week, we thank Story Coaches Jennie Eng and Alison Klein. Jennie and Alison are quick with their wit, generous with their time, and open with their hearts. They brought both laughter and compassion to these writers. We are lucky to count them members of this team.

For the striking photography throughout this book we thank Shout Mouse Photo Coach and Shootback founder Lana Wong. Lana helped these writers capture powerful portraits that portrayed *The Real You.* We are grateful for her dedication and her vision. We're thankful, too, for the smart graphic design work of Zoe Gatti, who designed the cover.

None of this work would have been possible without a generous grant from the HMFC fund, for which we are incredibly grateful. The folks behind this fund introduced us to Ballou and served as constant encouragement and support.

And most of all we thank these thirty dedicated writers who gave up lunch periods and stayed after school, always driven by the power of sharing their story with readers who needed to hear it. The selflessness and courage and tremendous strength of these authors will stay with us. We are so proud. Writing with—and learning from—these incredible teens was such a gift, and a joy.

—*Kathy Crutcher*
Founder, Shout Mouse Press

ABOUT SHOUT MOUSE PRESS

www.ShoutMousePress.org

Shout Mouse Press is a writing program and publishing house for unheard voices.

Shout Mouse was founded in Washington, DC in 2014. We partner with nonprofit organizations serving communities in need and design book projects that give voice to those communities and help further the nonprofits' missions. Shout Mouse authors have produced original children's books, memoir collections, and novels-in-stories.

We Believe

We believe everyone has a story to tell. We believe everyone has the ability to tell it. We believe by listening to the stories we tell each other—whether true or imagined, of hopes or heartbreaks or fantasies or fears—we are learning empathy, diplomacy, reflection, and grace. We believe we need to see ourselves in the stories we are surrounded by. We believe this is especially true for those who are made to believe that their stories do not matter: the poor or the sick or the marginalized or the battered. We feel lucky to be able to help unearth these stories, and we are passionate about sharing these unheard voices with the world.

ABOUT SHOOTBACK

www.ShootBackProject.org

Shootback empowers young people to tell their own stories and express their creative voices through photography, writing, and critical thinking about the world around them. Shootback started in Nairobi, Kenya in 1997 by putting cameras in the hands of teens from Mathare, one of Africa's largest slums, and culminated in the publication of *Shootback: Photos by Kids from the Nairobi Slums,* a documentary film, and an international traveling exhibition. Seventeen years on, Shootback continues to train a new generation of young photographers and now runs after-school programming in DC public schools in collaboration with various nonprofit organizations.

Shout Mouse Press is proud to partner with the Shootback team, who coach our authors to produce striking original photography for our books.

SHOOTBACK

FOR TEENS / ADULTS

THE BALLOU STORY PROJECT
by the students of Ballou Senior High School

The writers of Ballou High School in Southeast DC are working to Change the Narrative about young people of color in this country. Through their raw and powerful memoirs they challenge their readers to listen, and to recognize in each story a common humanity worthy of dignity, support, and respect.

TRINITOGA: STORIES OF LIFE IN A ROUGHED-UP, TOUGH-LOVE, NO-GOOD HOOD
by the young women of Beacon House

It's a roughed up hood, but we all got tough love for each other. So begins *Trinitoga*, a novel-in-stories by middle-school authors of Beacon House. These young writers created a fictionalized neighborhood and populated it with an endearing and heartbreaking cast of characters.

FOR CHILDREN

BOOKS BY TEENS SERIES
by the tutors of Reach Incorporated

As elementary school reading tutors in underserved communities in Washington, DC, the teens of Reach Incorporated noticed that few children's books reflected their reality. They decided to do something about that: they wrote their own.

HAITI'S FREEDOM WRITERS
by the young women of Restavek Freedom Foundation

Fifteen young women in Port-au-Prince were issued a challenge: use the power of story to help end child slavery in Haiti. These books aim to instill empathy for exploited children, create outrage at the injustice, and provide inspiration to stand up, speak up, and make a change.

Made in the USA
San Bernardino, CA
14 July 2015

A RIOT OF VOICES

Through the course of a historic year of civil unrest and the emergence of the #BlackLivesMatter Movement, thirty teen writers from Frank W. Ballou High School in Washington, DC came together to join this national conversation about race, inequality, violence, and justice. Through their powerful, personal stories these writers intend to Change the Story about youth of color. We are not thugs, they say. We are not victims. We are big sisters and sports stars, academic strivers and everyday heroes. We speak out for justice. We dream big dreams. These writers want more for themselves, more for their community, more for their generation. And they are challenging their readers to listen, and to recognize in each story a common humanity worthy of dignity, support, and respect. This riot of voices must be heard.

PRAISE FOR THE BALLOU STORY PROJECT, VOL. 1: *HOW TO GROW UP LIKE ME*

"One hour after I displayed the book *How to Grow up Like Me* in our middle school library, it was seized upon by an 8th grade boy who is a reluctant reader… and had only checked out one other book while in middle school. He made an instant connection with the honest and powerful stories written inside. This student ran down to show the book to his reading teacher. He is now captivated and can't wait to come to class to read the stories of these courageous authors. This is a great victory. Thank you for sharing this inspiring collection with our students. This is real. This is life-changing."
—Librarian, Hardy Middle School, Washington, DC

"I was so inspired by the powerful stories published by your students from Ballou! The narrative is so similar to my students here in Memphis and so many kids from urban school districts around the country. There is a need for a writing project like this here. Our students just don't have as many opportunities as they should to express how they feel and to be listened to."
—Teach For America instructor, Memphis, TN

SHOUT MOUSE PRESS

www.ShoutMousePress.org

ISBN 9780692455388

9 780692 455388